This book belongs to

....

....

Hi my name is Margaret. I'm named after St. Margaret of Antioch. Her symbol is a dragon's head holding a cross. This can be found in the King's Lynn coat of arms!

First published 2015

Copyright © Lindsey Bavin and Rebecca Rees, 2015

Lindsey Bavin and Rebecca Rees have asserted their right to be identified as the authors of this Work in accordance with the Copyright, Designs and Patents Act 1988

Every reasonable effort has been made to contact copyright holders of material reproduced in this book. If any have inadvertently been overlooked, the authors would be glad to hear from them and make good in future editions any errors or omissions brought to their attention.

ISBN 978-1-910693-51-3

Printed and bound by www.printondemand-worldwide.com

Sponsors

The Charity of William Cleave

Sir Jeremy Bagge

The Audrey Stratford Charitable Trust

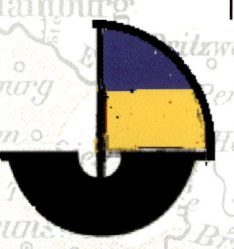

Marriott's Warehouse Trust

King's Lynn Hanseatic Club

Margaret Taylor

Soroptimist International
SI King's Lynn

Table of Contents

Foreword..5

Greetings from the Hanseatic League...6

Timeline..9

Chapter One: What is the Hanseatic League?......................................11

Chapter Two: Easterlings in Medieval Lynn..18

Chapter Three: Lynn Merchants Sail East..27

Chapter Four: Pirates, War and Peace in the 15th Century..................34

Chapter Five: Lynn and the Hanse Today..53

Activities...57

German Vocabulary..66

Glossary..67

Selected Bibliography...69

Acknowledgements...70

List of Illustrations..71

Hanse Festival Fireworks and Kamper Kogge. Images courtesy of The King's Lynn and West Norfolk Borough Council.

> Hi my name is Nick! I'm named after St Nicholas the patron saint of the Hanseatic League.
>
> Are you ready to explore our town's history?

Foreword

In 2015 King's Lynn celebrates 10 years as a member of the New Hanseatic League embracing 185 towns across northern Europe. During International Hanse Day in May a History and Archaeology Symposium (HAS) was organised by a group representing King's Lynn Hanseatic Club, Marriott's Warehouse Trust, True's Yard Fisherfolk Museum and the King's Lynn Town Guides. Four lecturers addressed full audiences on Hanseatic Archaeology and History at Marriott's Warehouse. The proceedings will be published in 2016 to allow more people to access them.

HAS is also the group responsible for this book. We would like school children in King's Lynn and West Norfolk to know more about the significance of the Hanseatic League in our town's story. Lynn played a prominent role in the overseas trade of the English nation before 1600. Its connections with the Low Countries and France were important but those with the German cities of the North Sea and Baltic more so.

Children will hopefully learn and enjoy this pioneer book as they discover Lynn's exceptional maritime past which generates civic pride and a strong sense of local identity. I thank all those involved in making it possible. The authors have engaged teachers and school children as well as the mayors of several Hanseatic towns. We are also grateful to our sponsors whose financial support has been essential to ensure this publication.

With best wishes

Dr Paul Richards FSA DL

Project Consultant

September 2015.

Greetings from the Hanseatic League

It was a great privilege for me to make the application for King's Lynn to join the New Hanse League and since then to have become the National Commissioner representing English towns to the Hanse League.

Playing such an active role in the Hanse League and working closely with local historian, Dr Paul Richards, has opened my eyes to the amazing history of the League, King's Lynn's place within it, and the opportunities available to our lovely town that being a part of the New League brings.

Being a member of such important international body helps promote King's Lynn across Europe and further afield and means that many more people are aware of our beautiful, historic town and the excellent quality of life it offers for those of us who live here.

I know you will enjoy, as I did, learning of the history of the Hanse League, the part that King's Lynn has played in that history, and indeed the part we continue to play as a community.

Please enjoy this book and perhaps play your own part in promoting our fantastic heritage.

Yours sincerely,

Nick Daubney
Leader of the Borough Council of King's Lynn and West Norfolk and the National Commissioner of England

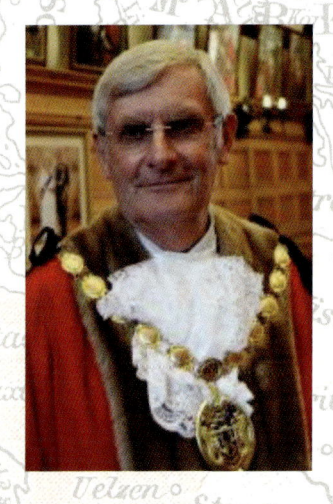

As Mayor of the Borough of King's Lynn and West Norfolk, it gives me the greatest pleasure to send you my greetings. Here in King's Lynn we have a population of 40,000 and are very proud indeed to be the first English town to have become a member of the New Hanseatic League in 2005. We look forward to continuing to play our part over the years as the League develops.

Since I was a child I have always looked forward to visiting a library and I am so pleased that young people still like reading and I do hope you find this book both interesting and enjoyable.

Councillor Colin Manning
Mayor of King's Lynn and West Norfolk

Greetings from Boston your sister town in Lincolnshire on the other side of the Wash. About 70,000 people live here.

We have just joined the New Hanseatic League in June. We are looking forward to working closely with you to make the League even better.

I hope you enjoy reading this book.

Councillor Richard Austin
The Worshipful Mayor of Boston and Admiral of the Wash

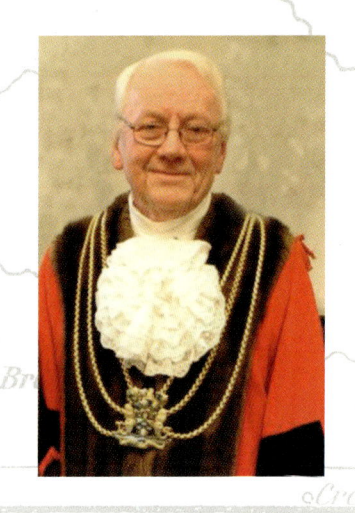

Greetings.

For me it is a great joy to greet all young readers as the mayor of the Hanseatic City of Lübeck and the Foreman of the Hanseatic League. It is terrific to see that young people are interested in the historical and modern Hanseatic League.

The "new" Hanseatic League has set itself the task of keeping alive the spirit of the League as a social and cultural alliance. By cultivating traditions and encouraging a vibrant exchange between its members, the League aims to bring about closer economic, cultural, social and national ties across Europe.

Lübeck was from the beginning the heart and the mind of the Hanseatic League, her pulse flowed through all cities and shaped their thinking. For this reason, Lübeck received the unofficial title "Queen of the Hanseatic League". Today, the Hanseatic City of Lübeck is a modern and international metropolis in northern Germany with about 215,000 inhabitants. The importance of Lübeck in history is still felt in many places including the medieval old town, a UNESCO World Heritage Site since 1987.

I invite all readers of this book to walk in the footsteps of the Hanseatic merchants and to feel the spirit of solidarity across national borders.

Lübeck, September 2015

Bernd Saxe
Mayor of the Hanseatic City of Lübeck and Foreman of the Hanseatic League

In 1241 Hamburg entered into a treaty with Lübeck, thereby becoming one of the founding cities of the Hanseatic League. It was in this context that we started trading with King's Lynn, so we have been trading partners for about 800 years. That's quite a long time, even by the impressive standards of European history.

Hamburg to this day calls itself "Free and Hanseatic City." It has 1,76 million inhabitants and is located in the north of Germany. We have the second largest port in all of Europe. It handles around 900 large ships a year and provides 156 000 jobs in the greater metropolitan area.

In conclusion, I would like to send my regards to the children of King's Lynn:

"Beste Grüße an die Kinder von King's Lynn!"

Olaf Scholz
Erster Bürgermeister

Dear Hanseatic friends,

The Hanseatic city of Kampen in the Netherlands sends warmest greetings to all of you!

Due to its ideal location on the former "Zuiderzee" and the mouth of the River IJssel, Kampen was a very important harbour town in the 14th and 15th century. Our Kogge ships sailed to many other Hanseatic cities, mostly in the Baltic, but also to King's Lynn. Maybe you saw the replica of our Kogge when it visited the Hanseatic Festival in your town recently?

Nowadays Kampen is a city with over 50.000 inhabitants. We joined the New Hanseatic League in 1980. In 2017 we will be proud to host the 37th International Hanseatic Days. If you want to learn more about our city please visit our website: www.kampen.nl or find more information on Wikipedia.

I hope you can come and visit us someday!

Yours faithfully,

Bort Koelewijn
Mayor of Kampen

Timeline

1086	The completion of William the Conqueror's Domesday Book, this contains the first written record of Lynn's existence.
1101	Lynn is recognised as a settlement by Bishop Losinga of Norwich and he founds St. Margaret's Church (Lynn Minster).
1140s	The second part of the town is founded and called the Newland; this included the Tuesday Market Place and St. Nicholas Chapel.
1204	Lynn is granted its first royal charter of borough freedom by King John. By this time Lynn is one of the five largest ports in England.
1260s	The river Great Ouse is diverted from Wisbech to Lynn.
1348	The Black Death kills over half of Lynn's population (and about half the population of England).
1356	The Hanseatic League's first Congress (or Hansetag) is held in Lübeck.
1468-1474	England is at war with the Hanseatic League.
1474	The Treaty of Utrecht – Edward IV grants the Hanseatic League a property in Lynn as part of a peace treaty between England and the Hanseatic League.

1475	Lynn's Hanseatic Kontor (the Hanse House) is built.
1530s	Henry VIII's Reformation – the friaries of Lynn are largely demolished, with the towers of the Greyfriars and Whitefriars left standing as seamarks.
1537	Henry VIII takes control of Lynn from the Bishops of Norwich. The town changes its name from Bishop's Lynn (Lynn Episcopi) to King's Lynn (Lynn Regis).
1560s	The Hanseatic merchants leave Lynn for London.
1643	The Civil War comes to Lynn and the town spends 3 weeks under siege from Parliamentarian forces which include Oliver Cromwell.
1741	The Great Gale blows down the spires of St. Margaret's Church and St. Nicholas Chapel.
1751	The Hanseatic League sells the Hanse House to a family of Lynn merchants.
1980	The New Hanseatic League is formed.
2004	Hanseatic Festival and Kieler Kogge visited Lynn.
2005	Lynn joins the New Hanseatic League.
2009	St. Margaret's House is renamed The Hanse House and the Lisa von Lübeck visited Lynn.
2012	Hull joins the New Hanseatic League.
2015	Lynn celebrates the 10th anniversary of joining the New Hanseatic League and Boston also joins.

Chapter One:

What is The Hanseatic League?

First off, what is the Hanseatic League?

Well it says in this book...

The History of the Hanse

The Hanseatic League, also called Hansa or Hanse, was founded by northern German trading towns to protect their mutual economic interests. The Hanseatic League dominated commercial activity in northern Europe from the 13th to the 15th century...

Err what does that mean?

Well, if you were travelling somewhere new would you feel better going alone or with your friends?

"With friends?"

"Exactly, that is what they did. It's pretty simple when you think about it."

"Surely they'd only need to go with friends the first time? Then they'd know where they were going?"

"Well a lot could go wrong in Medieval Europe, so it was always safer to travel together."

Common Pitfalls of Travel

Pirates **Lice** **Plague** **Storms**

Did You Know? The word Hanse was a medieval German word and referred to a "guild" or "company".

*The first steps in the formation of the Hanseatic League took place in the second half of the 13th century. While overseas, the German **merchants** had tended increasingly to form "hanses" or groups in order to secure protection against robbers and pirates. They also built lighthouses at the entrances of ports to prevent wrecks and trained pilots in the art of navigation....*

Extent of the Hanseatic League

FUN FACT! The town wasn't always called King's Lynn, in fact it has had 3 different names. Its first name Lenne meant "lake or pool" and its second, Bishop's Lynn, was because the town was under the control of the Church.

The name King's Lynn came from Henry VIII in 1537 when the Norwich Bishops lost control of the town.

Glossary
Merchants – People who buy and sell things made by others for a profit.

"This is all very interesting, Nick, but what does this have to do with King's Lynn?"

"Let's keep reading Margaret! Maybe we will find out?"

*The first reference to the Hanseatic League in Lynn is in 1271, when German merchants secured **trading privileges**. It wasn't all smooth sailing because these privileges were not confirmed until 1310! Almost 30 years later!*

*All foreign merchants had to reside with Lynn **burgesses** but the Germans were allowed their own houses.*

"Can I read a bit? *Despite the fact that the majority of Hanseatic towns had little or nothing to do with England, the most important ones (Lübeck, Hamburg, Bremen, Cologne and Danzig) did.*
London and England's east coast ports were major trading partners of these German cities, with Lynn, Boston, Hull and Ipswich standing out."

Glossary
Trading privileges = Backstage Passes. Better treatment, no queues, might get to meet the band...ok maybe not the last one.
Burgess - A Burgess is a valued member of the community who has been given the Freedom of the Borough. (Originally it meant freedom from serfdom/ slavery).
Hinterland - Areas beyond a coastal district or river banks.

Did You Know? Lynn and Boston were prime destinations for Hanseatic merchants trying to establish themselves in the West, as they made up a large percentage of English imports and exports. These Wash ports attracted the German *Hanse* because their extensive **hinterlands** offered commercial opportunities and rewards with rich farmland, towns and cities.

Towns with historical ties to the Hanseatic League

As well as bringing Baltic fish and forest products to sell in the English market, north German merchants were attracted by the international fairs of the eastern counties, along with Italian, Spanish and Flemish men. Boston, Lynn, Stamford, Northampton and St Ives were the places to buy highly valued English wool in particular.

What English historians call the Hanseatic League made its formal entry onto the international stage as the German Hanse at the Congress or Hansetag in Lübeck in 1356. The desire of the Hanseatic cities to assert control over four great trading posts (Bergen, Bruges, Novgorod and London) abroad seems to have been the trigger. Then they were tested in war with Denmark in the 1360's for control of the Baltic. The German Hanse emerged victorious with the Treaty of Stralsund in 1370. The West now had to recognise that a new power had arisen in the North of Germany.

Did You Know? By 1400 the Hanseatic League claimed a membership of about 100 towns, mostly German. The League had no **constitution** and no permanent army, navy, or governing body except for occasional assemblies known as the *Hansetag (first held in* 1356). There was, however, no founding charter or official launch, even though Bremen asked Cologne to search the **archive** for one in 1418!

Glossary
Archive - A collection of historic documents.
Constitution - a set of rules which organise how a state or group is governed.

So from the sounds of it The Hanseatic League was formed to:

a) Make more money
b) Get added protection from pirates
c) Get more control over international trade.

Exactly! But it wasn't always smooth sailin. In 1468 war broke out between the English and the Hanseatic League and the merchants wouldn't return to Lynn until late 1474! By 1560 they deserted the town for London.

How many Germans were based at Lynn?

In a Lübeck customs list covering the five English ports (1474-81) Lynn was placed third behind Hull in the number of active Hanseatic traders (41 and 43 respectively). London was first with 76 merchants, but the Steelyard by the Thames probably accommodated many more before 1468.

Glossary
Steelyard – The name for the main trading post of the Hanseatic League in London.

Chapter Two:
Easterlings in Medieval Lynn

Who were the Easterlings?

This map shows where many Medieval European merchants came from to visit Lynn.

Glossary
Medieval - Also known as the Middle Ages this commonly refers to the period in European history between AD 600 and AD 1500.

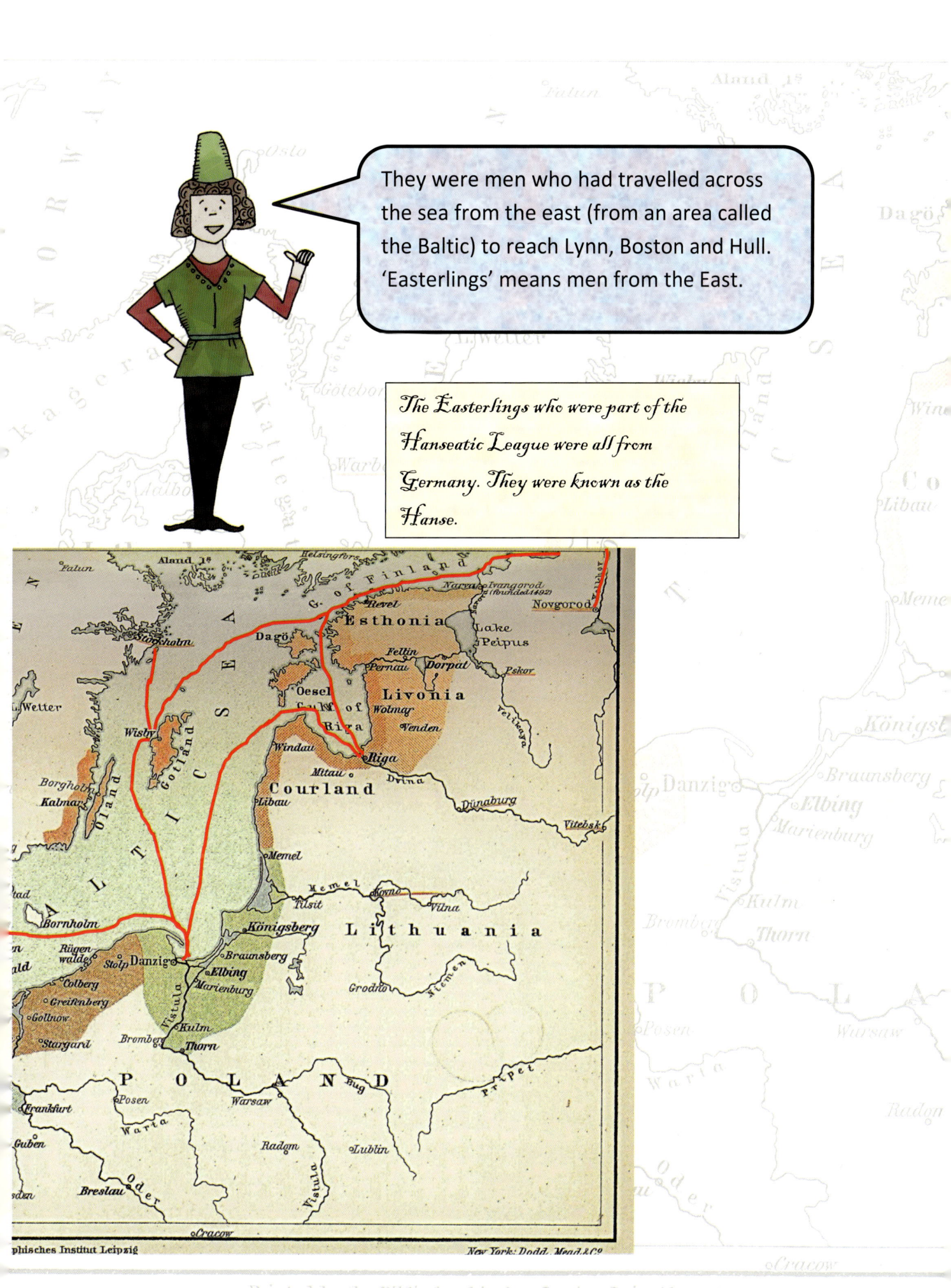

They were men who had travelled across the sea from the east (from an area called the Baltic) to reach Lynn, Boston and Hull. 'Easterlings' means men from the East.

The Easterlings who were part of the Hanseatic League were all from Germany. They were known as the Hanse.

"Why did they come to Lynn?"

"The location of Lynn was useful for international trade, as it is situated on England's east coast. It faces Europe across the North Sea. London and Scotland are also within fairly easy reach by ship."

*Through the River Ouse, its **tributaries** and the Fenland waterways, goods could be transported between Lynn and inland towns.*

King's Lynn

Ely

Cambridge

*The Hanse also received **commercial** privileges from England's kings. This meant they could make larger profits on their goods because they were not **taxed** very much on **imports** and **exports**.*

Glossary
Commercial – A business which makes money.
Export – Sending goods to another country to sell.
Import – Bringing goods in from abroad to sell.
Tax – An added cost to goods which has to be paid to the government.
Tributaries – Small rivers which flow into larger rivers.

What did the Hanse bring to Lynn?

They brought many things, one of which was fish. In the medieval period fish was a big part of peoples' diet.

FUN FACT! Stockfish is cod from Norway which has been hung on a rack and dried by the wind.

Stockfish (Cod)

Herring

Cod was often dried and herring was usually salted and transported in barrels.

Did You Know? The fish trade gave its name to one of Lynn's streets, Stockfish Row (now King Street) where fish merchants and fishmongers probably lived.

The local fishing fleet was based in the North End, and it supplied a lot of the fish which the people of Lynn ate. Lynn was also the source of fish for many towns inland, so to keep up with demand fish was also imported.

21

Pitch from the Baltic

Wine from France, Spain and Portugal

Timber from the Baltic

Soap from Bruges

Furs from Russia

Cloth from Bruges

Beeswax from the Baltic

Fabric dye from France

Glossary
Pitch – Can be used in its liquid form to waterproof wooden ships

The Hanse didn't just bring fish though. There were lots of other goods which they brought to Lynn!

Grain

Cloth

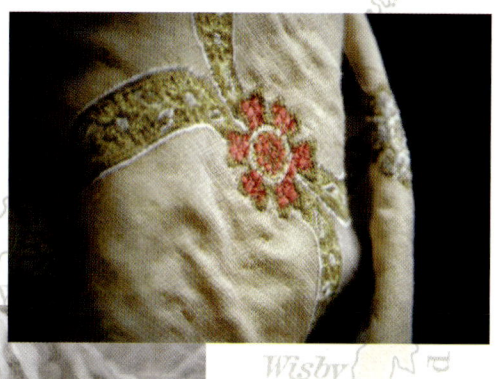

Salt

Wool

Beer

The Hanse also bought English goods to send home or to sell elsewhere.

Jettons were coin-like objects used by merchants as counters for calculating accounts.

Jetton, courtesy of West Norfolk and King's Lynn Archaeological Society © 2013

Did You Know? They also exported pottery made in Grimston. This pottery was green-glazed and often had bearded faces. Examples have been found as far away as Bergan.

> Wool was especially valuable for trading. Italians, **Flemings** and Germans came to Lynn to buy wool to send to Europe, where it was used to make high quality cloth.

> Most of these goods would have arrived in Lynn on ships, called **cogs**, packed in barrels. Cloth and furs were wrapped in bundles, while wool, salt and grain were transported in sacks.

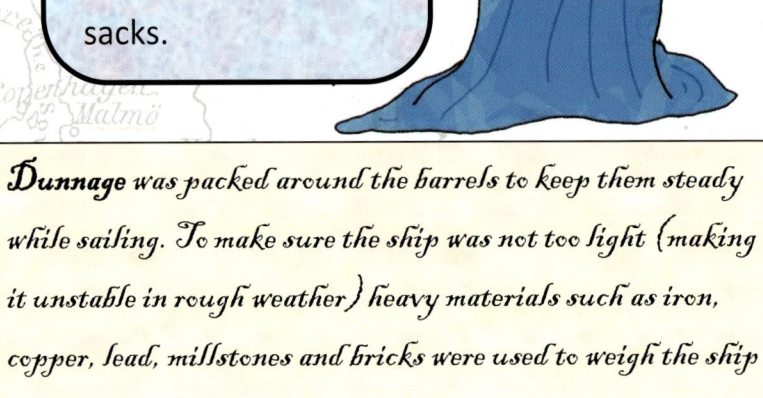

Did You Know? Wool sacks usually weighed about 26 tons each and needed four men to move them.

Dunnage was packed around the barrels to keep them steady while sailing. To make sure the ship was not too light (making it unstable in rough weather) heavy materials such as iron, copper, lead, millstones and bricks were used to weigh the ship down.

Warehouses in Lynn, like those attached to the Hanse House, were used to store and sell the goods. Both the Trinity and St George's Guildhalls also had warehouses and cellars for storage. They were in the town centre and next to the grand houses of wealthy merchants and the market places.

Glossary
Cogs – Ships with a single mast and a square sail [German – **Kogge**]
Dunnage – Loose material used to secure cargo on a journey.
Flemings/Flemish – People from North Belgium.

FUN FACT! Cats were kept on board to stop rats eating the grain.

What impact did the Hanse have on the people of Lynn?

The Hanseatic influence in 14th century Lynn is clear from the two large Flemish brasses in St. Margaret's Church. These are life-sized images of two local merchants and their wives.

When people came into St. Margaret's they must have been impressed by these wonderful memorials which showed how important the merchants were. Their families also hoped townspeople would pray for these merchants.

The brasses would once have had coloured beeswax pressed into the lines and they would have been polished. These were very expensive memorials to have made and imported from abroad.

After 1400, as London's trade with the Hanseatic League grew, trade with east coast ports such as Lynn and Boston declined. They still remained two of England's largest and richest towns in the 14th to 15th centuries, hosting a large number of German merchants.

```
Port Bailiff Arrest Report
Date: 1408.
Name: Nicholas Warpull.
Occupation: Prussian ship
captain from Danzig.
Crime: Failure to pay local
cloth merchant, John Patryk.
Action: The Mayor assembled
Lynn burgesses and foreign
sailors on one of Lynn's
quays. John Patryk was
questioned and supported by a
dyer and a goldsmith.
Outcome: Debt paid.
Notes: Accused three years
ago of stealing four anchors
from a Lynn merchant ship in
Marstrand (Norway).
```

Did You Know? The **Kontor** became known as St. Margaret's House, until 2009, when it was renamed The Hanse House to highlight its history.

In 1561 the Hanseatic League left Lynn. They kept possession of their Lynn Kontor until 1751, when they sold it to a family of wealthy Lynn merchants.

What happened to the Hanse?

Glossary
Bailiff – An officer who collects money owed.
Burgess – Someone in a town or borough with full rights of citizenship.
Kontor – A foreign trading post of the Hanseatic League, which contained offices, storage and living space.
Prussia – An area of Northern Europe.

Chapter Three:

Lynn Merchants Sail East

So what do we know about Lynn merchants who travelled to Hanseatic cities?

Well, one merchant was the son of Margery Kempe. He married a woman from Danzig and they had a daughter. While they were visiting Margery in Lynn her son died. Margery's daughter-in-law stayed with her for over a year, before deciding to go home.

Margery, aged about 55 (old for then!), joined her daughter-in-law on her journey back to Danzig. They sailed from Ipswich, but bad storms at sea forced them to land in Norway before finishing their journey.

I then went on **pilgrimage** to Wilsnack (in Germany). I travelled first by boat, then on foot. I returned to Lynn after four months away, having been abandoned by my travelling companions, visited countries at war with England and caught lice!

Did You Know? Margery's autobiography, *The Book of Margery Kempe*, was the first written in English. Margery couldn't read or write so she had to dictate it to a Lynn friar.

Glossary
Pilgrimage – A journey to visit a religious site or object.

"Many Lynn merchants would have travelled abroad, often on Hanseatic ships, when they went on pilgrimage."

"People usually went on a pilgrimage when they needed forgiveness from God for their sins. They believed that visiting holy sites or **relics** meant they would reach Heaven quicker when they died."

*Pilgrims often returned home with souvenirs from the different **shrines** they had visited – these are called Pilgrims' Badges.*

Pilgrims' Badges: Courtesy of Lynn Museum, Norfolk Museums Service.

"Many pilgrims also arrived in Lynn from all over Europe on their way to the shrine at Walsingham. I went abroad to the Holy Land, Rome and Santiago."

Did You Know? Walsingham and Canterbury Cathedral were the two most important medieval shrines in England.

Glossary
Relics – Objects connected to religious figures; such as bones, blood or wood (from Jesus' cross).
Shrines – Holy places dedicated to someone (usually religious).

"John Brown was another Lynn merchant. He delivered letters from King Henry IV to Hanseatic cities. He also hosted foreign politicians in his home."

"Lynn merchants had useful connections with Hanseatic cities which made them valuable **diplomatically**. They knew and understood the people who lived there."

These links between Lynn and Hanseatic merchants were tested during the 1380s when both sides started seizing the other's ships and confiscating their cargoes in Danzig and England.

This disrupted business and meant the merchants were losing money. The merchants of Lynn submitted a claim for damages of about £2000 – and that was after it had been halved!

Diplomatically – To be involved in peace or treaty talks.

Was it safe for Lynn merchants to travel abroad?

No it wasn't! Lynn merchant ships travelled in groups (or convoys) as protection against pirates. Sailing across the North Sea was so risky that no one owned a whole ship, instead they owned a portion of it (called a share).

These shares were often given to people as presents. Owning only part of a ship meant you would not lose everything if the ship sank in a storm or was attacked by pirates.

King's Lynn Borough Archives: KL/C 2/35, image courtesy of the Norfolk Record Office.

The ships which Lynn merchants would have sailed in were called cogs. They were easily recognizable by their single mast and single square sail.

Left: *This cog was drawn in the initial 'H' on letters detailing rights granted to the borough of Lynn by Henry VI in 1441. The word 'Lenn' (Lynn) appears on the ship's sail.*

A Medieval Ship

Crow's nest: This allows the crew to keep watch for land and pirates!

Main sail: A single square sail which catches the wind to power the ship through the sea.

Main mast: The tallest mast, located near the centre of the ship; it carries the sail and rigging.

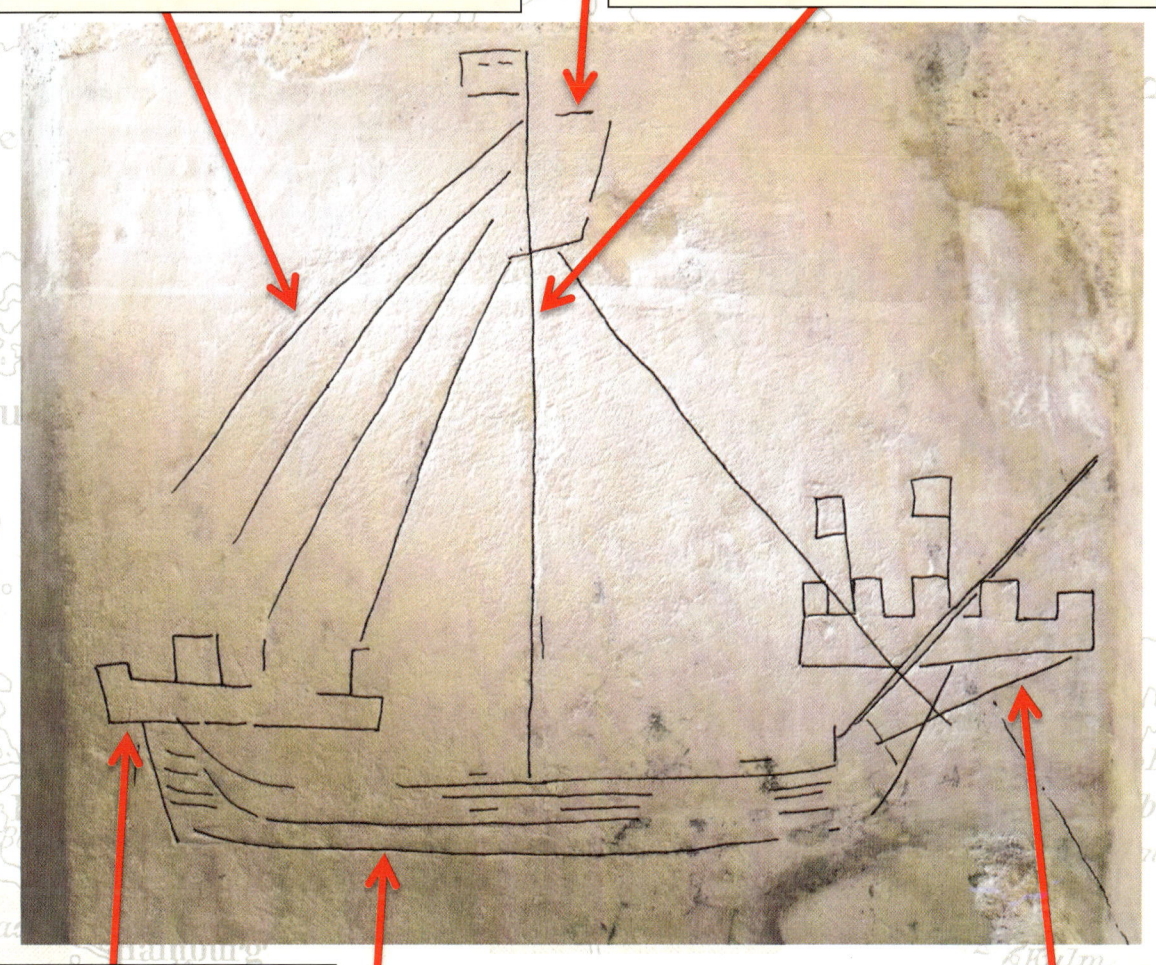

Ship graffiti from St. Margaret's church, Cley next the Sea, Norfolk, © Norfolk Medieval Graffiti Survey.

The bow: The front of the ship has been built up to form a 'castle'. This makes the ship easier to defend with archers.

The stern: The back of the ship has also been built up to form a 'castle'. The ship was steered from here using a rudder.

The hull: The body of the ship where cargo is stored.

Did You Know? The ship's crew would have slept on deck, probably under canvas shelters. Sometimes, because sea sickness was common, they landed and slept ashore.

Lynn merchants abroad also had to deal with an organisation called The Teutonic Knights (known as the Deutscher Orden).

They started off as warrior monks in Jerusalem but when the Pope asked them, in the 13th century, to bring Christianity to Eastern Europe, the Teutonic Knights instead conquered areas of land and created **Prussia**.

The Knights were the only territorial (non-city) member of the Hanseatic League but they had ships and traded like merchants. They also protected merchants, cargo and land (such as *Gotland*) from pirates.

Membership of the Teutonic Knights was mainly German and they were ruled by a Grand Master, who was based in a large castle at Marienburg (now in Poland).

Glossary
Gotland – Sweden's largest island

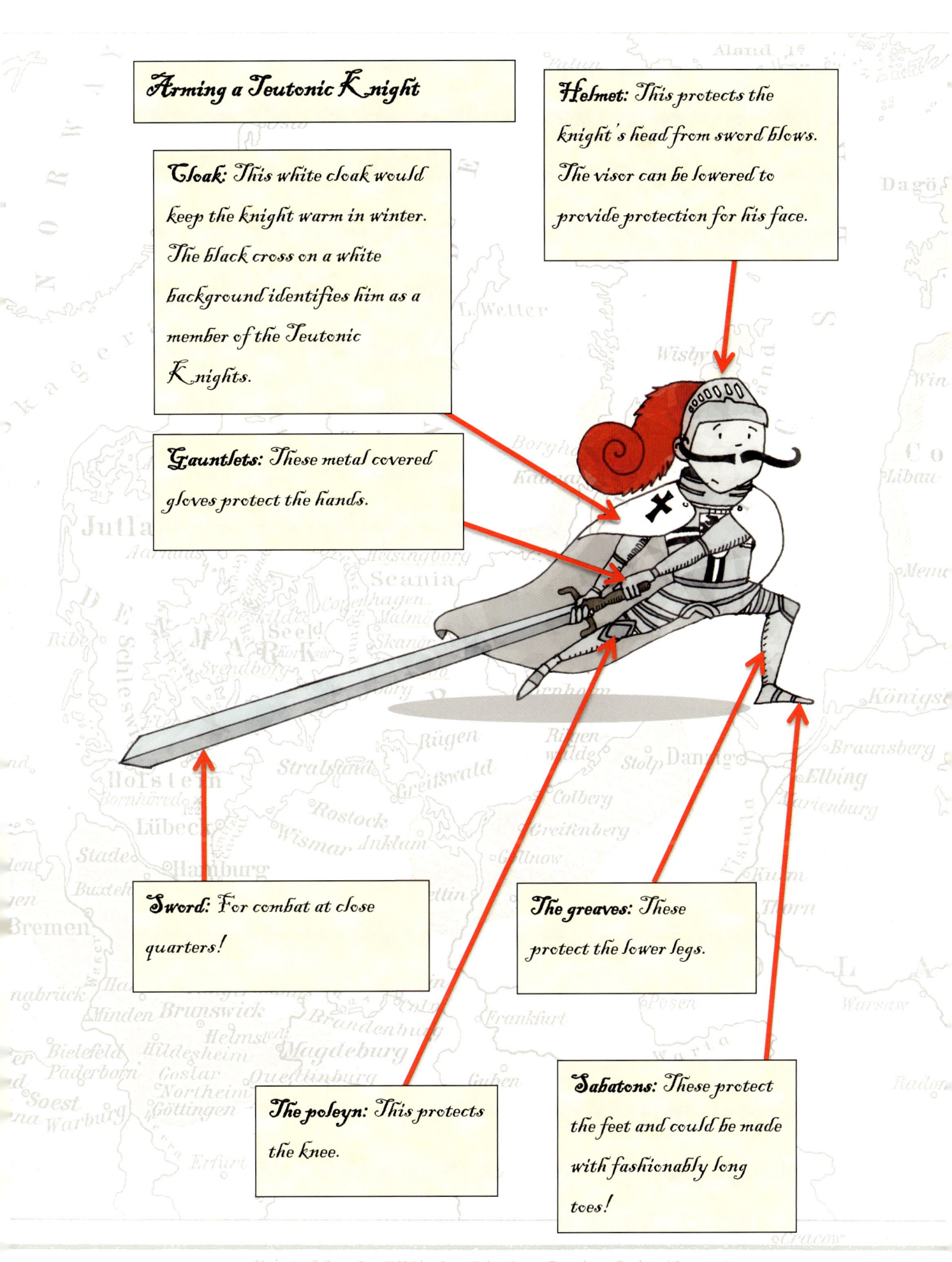

Arming a Teutonic Knight

Cloak: This white cloak would keep the knight warm in winter. The black cross on a white background identifies him as a member of the Teutonic Knights.

Helmet: This protects the knight's head from sword blows. The visor can be lowered to provide protection for his face.

Gauntlets: These metal covered gloves protect the hands.

Sword: For combat at close quarters!

The greaves: These protect the lower legs.

The poleyn: This protects the knee.

Sabatons: These protect the feet and could be made with fashionably long toes!

Chapter Four:
Pirates, War and Peace in the 15th Century
Part 1
Trouble in Iceland and Norway
Norway

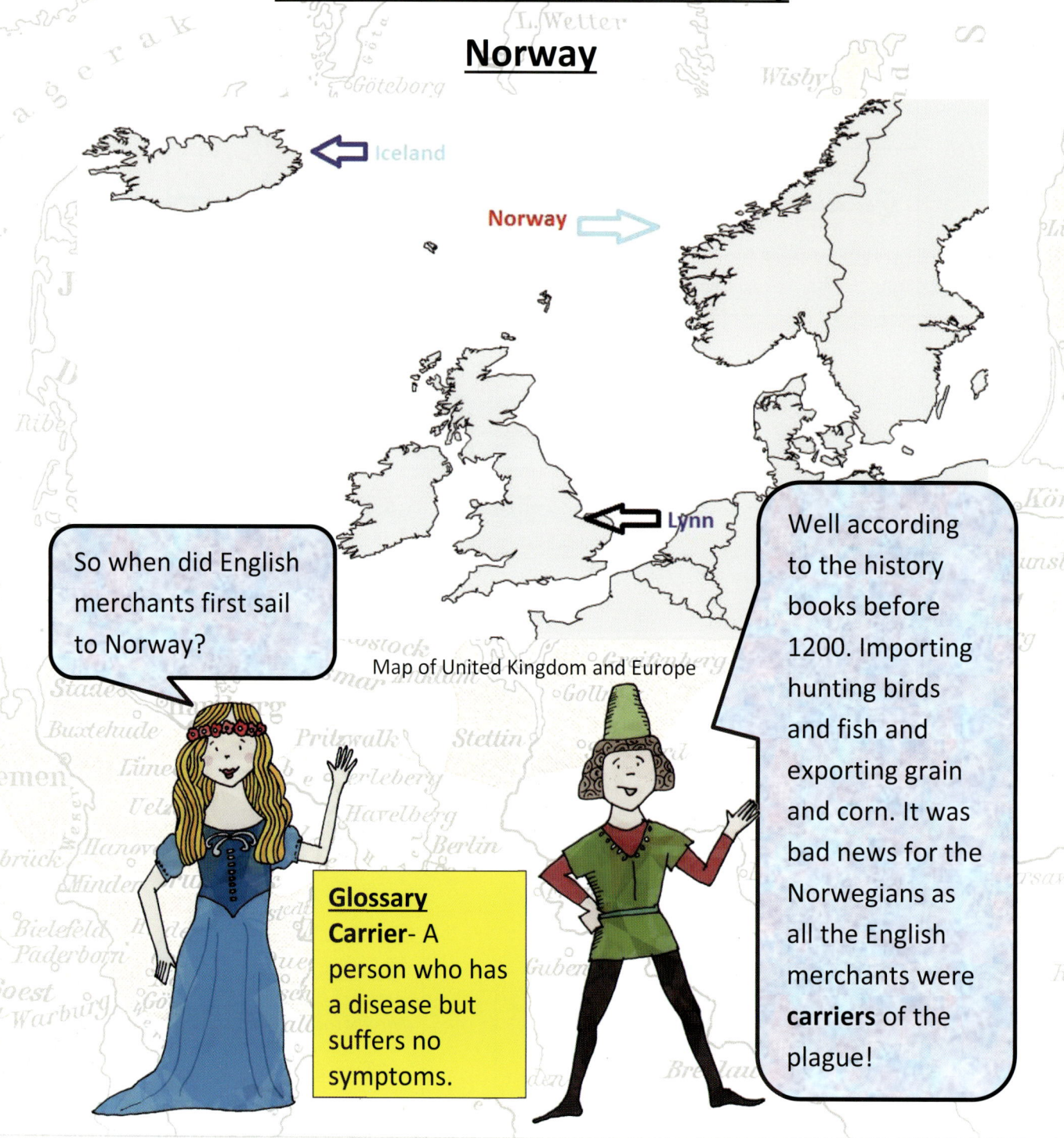

Map of United Kingdom and Europe

So when did English merchants first sail to Norway?

Well according to the history books before 1200. Importing hunting birds and fish and exporting grain and corn. It was bad news for the Norwegians as all the English merchants were carriers of the plague!

Glossary
Carrier- A person who has a disease but suffers no symptoms.

Did You Know? The Plague also known as the 'Black Death' would go on to wipe out 60% of Europe's population by the end of the 14th Century.

Symptoms of the Plague:

- Headache
- Chills
- Fever
- **Buboes**

Were the Hanse merchants also in Norway at that time?

Yes, they had a **kontor** in Bergen but conflict meant it was abandoned in 1368-69. In their **absence** the English merchants moved in and built their own warehouses.

What happened when the Hanse merchants came back?

The Norwegians were worried about the English. King Erik of Norway gave the merchants their own guard to protect them.

Glossary
Buboes- Inflammation of the lymph nodes in the armpit and groin.
Kontor- Trading post.
Absence- To be gone.

Timeline of events in Norway

1368 - Hanseatic Kontor abandoned.

1390 - £1094 worth of stockfish brought to Lynn from Bergen.

1393 - 17 ships from Lynn are recorded as being in Bergen

22nd April 1393 - Vitalien Brotherhood attacked Bergen, 21 houses were burnt down and they caused £1814 worth of damage.

1402 - German merchants were summoned before King Eric's court and told they would have to pay **compensation** if English subjects were harmed.

1406 - Norfolk fishermen killed by Hamburg merchants off the coast of Norway.

1411 - Hanse merchants banned from Norway.

1411 - English merchants thrived; Thomas Cross and John Foullere from Lynn took on **apprentices**.

Did You Know? Henry IV came to Lynn with his daughter Phillipa who would sail to Norway to wed King Eric. They stayed in Lynn for 9 days. This union secured **commercial privileges** for the English in Bergen.

Glossary
Compensation- Money given as a formal apology.
Commercial Privileges- Special benefits like paying less tax.
Apprentices- Young people learning a particular craft.

The Life of an Apprentice in Bergen

Dear Dad,

The Baltic Sea, 23rd August 1474

I'm not sure when you'll get this, the Captain said he'd drop my letters off when he next sails into Lynn. Wouldn't it be nice if there a special delivery just for letters so they'd reach you quicker!

We've been at sea for almost a month now, the Captain said it won't be much longer which is a relief as all the food's gone stale and half the crew have got scurvy! Last night when I was swabbing the deck I found 15 teeth!

Love

Peter

PS Thanks for the socks.

Ewww!

Did You Know? Scurvy is caused by a lack of Vitamin C and was a serious condition for sailors. The lack of fresh fruit and vegetables caused many to suffer lethargy, erratic mood swings, shortness of breath, bleeding gums and yes even tooth loss!

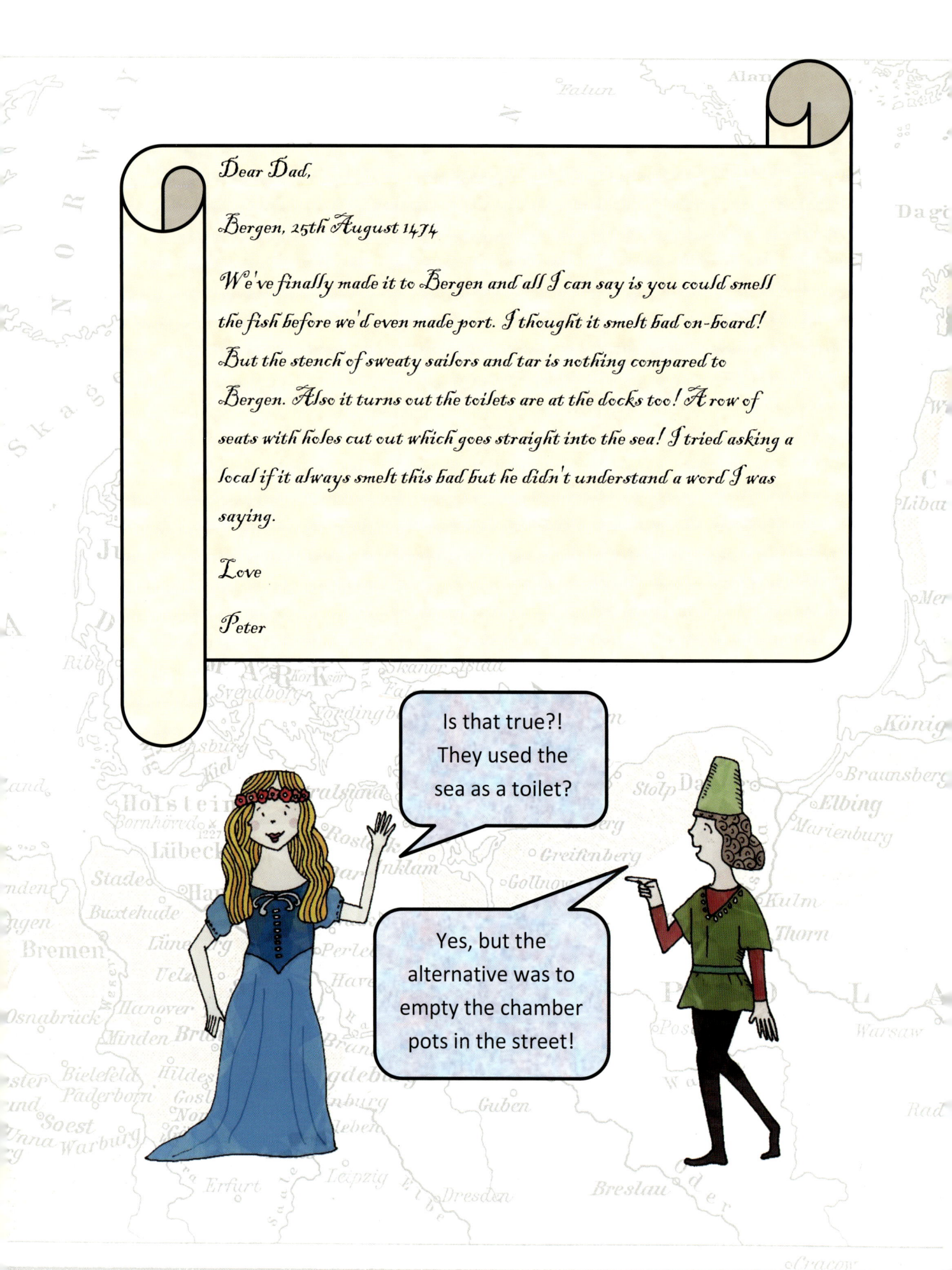

Dear Dad,

Bergen, 25th August 1474

We've finally made it to Bergen and all I can say is you could smell the fish before we'd even made port. I thought it smelt bad on-board! But the stench of sweaty sailors and tar is nothing compared to Bergen. Also it turns out the toilets are at the docks too! A row of seats with holes cut out which goes straight into the sea! I tried asking a local if it always smelt this bad but he didn't understand a word I was saying.

Love

Peter

Is that true?! They used the sea as a toilet?

Yes, but the alternative was to empty the chamber pots in the street!

Dear Dad,

Bergen, 26th August 1474

Officially started work as an apprentice today, the hours are long and the work is hard but I only have to share my bed with one other apprentice, so it's not like back home! I say bed, it is actually a cupboard, but it's warm and dry so can't complain.

Learned an important lesson today, one of the boys smuggled a candle in as he was afraid of the dark. The foreman found it and was absolutely furious. Apparently candles are strictly forbidden because of the risk of fire.

Love Peter

Did You Know? Duties for an apprentice includes cooking the large cauldrons of porridge for the workers, chopping vegetables, scrubbing floors and tables, lifting and carrying heavy goods. As well as learning the trade to which they were apprenticed.

Dear Dad,

Bergen, 30th October 1474

Remember the boy who brought in a candle? I thought the beating he was given by the foreman would be the end of it but no! There's a book where an apprentice's bad behaviour is recorded and the tenement court is holding a trial for any apprentice who has broken the rules. Those who have been naughty will receive as many beatings as the court sees fit. The foreman used a tarred rope but the court here uses a bullwhip. Apparently this is known as being paid in "High German Shillings".

Love Peter

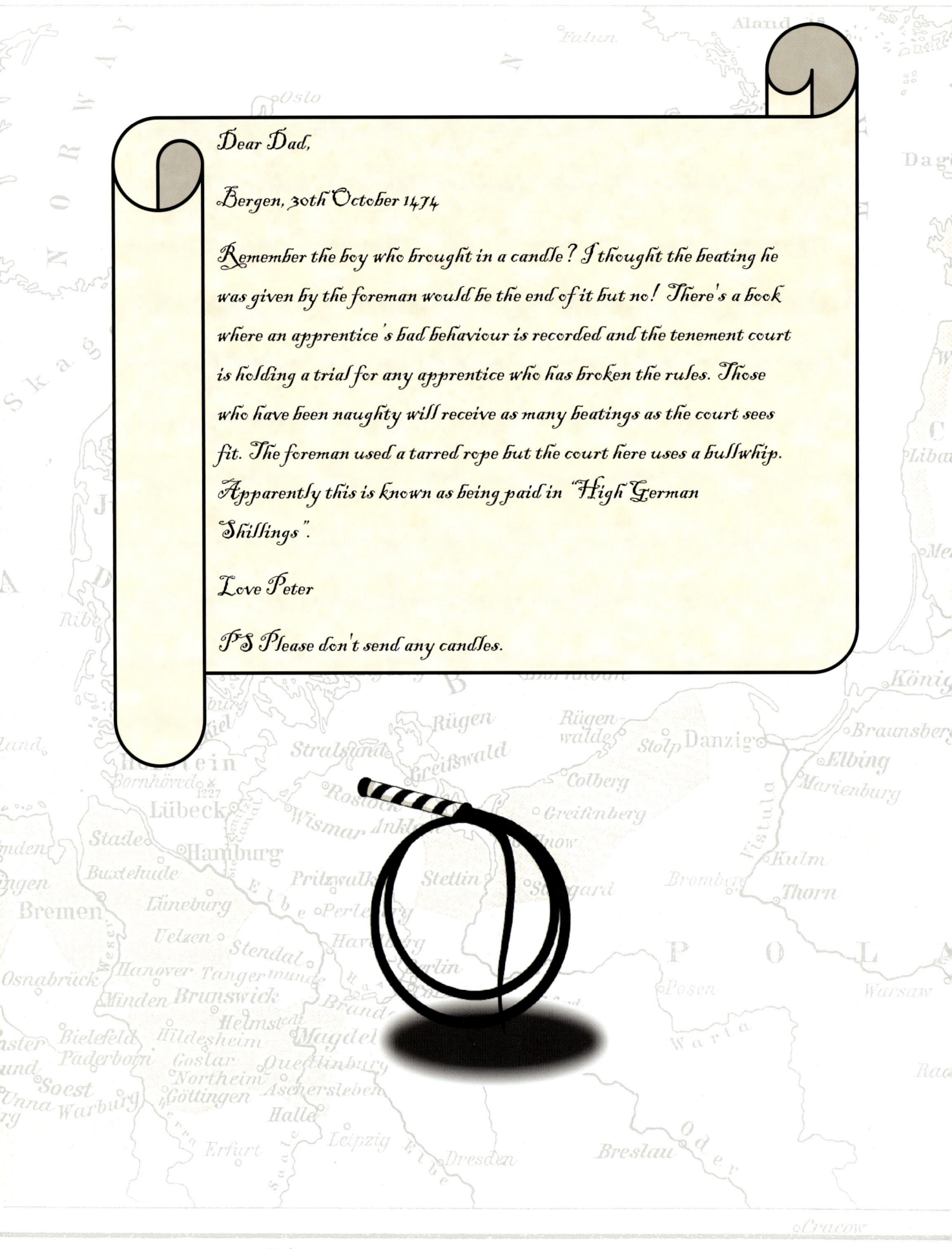

PS Please don't send any candles.

Iceland

> It's very far away. What attracted English merchants to Iceland?

> Loads of things- honey, butter, grain, beer, needles and even shoes!

Timeline of Iceland

1415 – King Eric wrote to Lynn to complain about Norfolk fishermen and traders going to Iceland to avoid paying taxes. He banned fishing for 12 months in Danish, Norwegian or Icelandic waters.

1419 - 25 English merchant ships were lost in 1419 in a single storm.

1424 - The mayors of Lynn, Yarmouth, Hull and Newcastle all petitioned against the proclamation. Henry IV raised grievances of Lynn men with King Erik. Erik and the Bishop of Iceland accused the English of murdering his Danish governor Palsson and Lynn merchants kidnapping Icelandic children.

1427 - Although they denied kidnapping the children, promises were made to return them to Iceland.

1432 - Anglo-Danish treaty was signed and peace restored.

1460 - Icelanders living peacefully in Lynn, Hull and Bristol.

Part 2

Pirates in the North Sea and Baltic

I love pirates! Give me a moment, I'm going to get changed!

Did You Know? The Hanseatic League put a tax on their members called "pfundzoll". The tax paid for "peace ships" which were armed with **mercenaries** to protect the merchant vessels. The Hanseatic League equipped a fleet of ships with 950 men!

Ok Margaret! In the 1370's and 1380's pirates were the **scourge** of the North Sea and the Baltic. It was the fear of them that **catalysed** the North German towns to act together for mutual protection.

But who were they defending against?

Glossary
Scourge- A menace
Catalysed- To start or trigger an event.
Mercenaries- Soldiers for hire.

42

The Vitalien Brotherhood

"God's friends and the whole world's enemies"
Vitalien Battle Cry

Facts about the Vitalien Brotherhood

- They began as privateers
- Originally hired by the Dukes of Mecklenburg to help the besieged city of Stockholm.
- The privateers brought vittles this is where the name came from.
- Turned to piracy in 1393
- Sacked 9 cities in the space of two years. Starting with Bergen.
- Captured Gotland in 1394

> Avast! Ye landlubbers! The Dread Pirate Margaret has arrived! The two pirate bands feared most were The Vitalien Brotherhood and The Likedeelers.

Did You Know? Appeals were made to King Richard II to help fight the pirates and Queen Margaret I of Denmark tried to charter English ships. She asked for three ships from Lynn. In 1398 Grand Master Konrad von Jungingen and his Teutonic Knights attacked and conquered the pirates and retook the island.

> Excellent knights are so much better than pirates, time for me to change!

> As if, pirates are so much better!

Glossary
Privateers - Legal pirates.
Vittles – Food or other supplies.
Sacked - To attack a city.
Gotland - An island in the Baltic Sea.

Pirates vs Knights

Be gone villains! The knights have arrived!

The German Order of Teutonic Knights were used by the Hanseatic League to battle the pirates. They were warrior monks founded in Acre in the late 12th century to provide hospital care for **crusaders** from the West. The **Teutonic** Order was invited by the Pope to bring Christianity to the pagan lands of Eastern Europe about 1220; it was not long before they had established their own state of Prussia. Their castle and HQ was at Marienburg south of Danzig.

FUN FACT! The Prussia of the Teutonic Knights was the only territorial member of the Hanseatic League and these warrior monks served the German Hanse as an armed force. Not least to clear the Baltic of pirates!

Glossary
Teutonic- German people or things.
Crusader- A Christian knight who fought in the Crusades to claim Jerusalem.
Prussia- The name of a country in Northern Europe.

Did You Know? The name Knights Templar was originally *Poor Knights of Christ and the Temple of Solomon* as their headquarters was located on the former site of the Temple of Solomon destroyed by the Romans in 70CE.

The Likedeelers

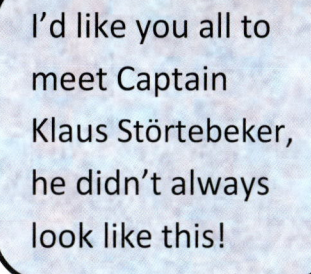

I'd like you all to meet Captain Klaus Störtebeker, he didn't always look like this!

Name: Klaus Störtebeker

Born: Wismar circa 1360

Died: Beheaded in Grasbrook, Hamburg, circa 1402

First appearance as a pirate: 1398

Crew: 73

Motto: "Everyman gets his share"

Other leaders: Gottfried Michaelson, Hennig Wichmann and Magister Wigbold.

Caught by- Mayor of Hamburg, Simon of Utrecht

Did You Know? The name Störtebeker translates as "down the beaker", which was Klaus' party trick- to down a beaker on one go! These weren't the tiny plastic cups we know today –a beaker at that time could contain up to 4 litres which is 7 pints of beer!

Any crewman of conquered ships who did not resist the pirates were thrown overboard, but if he did, he was treated fairly.

FUN FACT! Legend has it that Störtebeker offered his treasure to the Mayor of Hamburg in exchange for his freedom but the Mayor refused.

Another story is that Störtebeker bet the Mayor if he could walk past his men after being **beheaded** the Mayor would spare as many of his crewmen as he had walked past. After the fall of the axe Störtebeker's corpse was said to have walked past 11 of his crew before the **executioner** tripped him up!

The Execution of Klaus Störtebeker

Did You Know? Störtebeker's executioner was also beheaded- when asked if he was tired after **decapitating** 74 men he joked he could execute the entire **Senate** of Hamburg which, in hindsight, was a poor choice of words.

Glossary
Executioner- Person paid to legally kill people.
Beheaded/decapitating – Removal of a head.
Senate- A political governing body.

Printed by the Bibliographisches Institut Leipzig

Anglo-Hanseatic Sea War 1468-73

What really started the war?

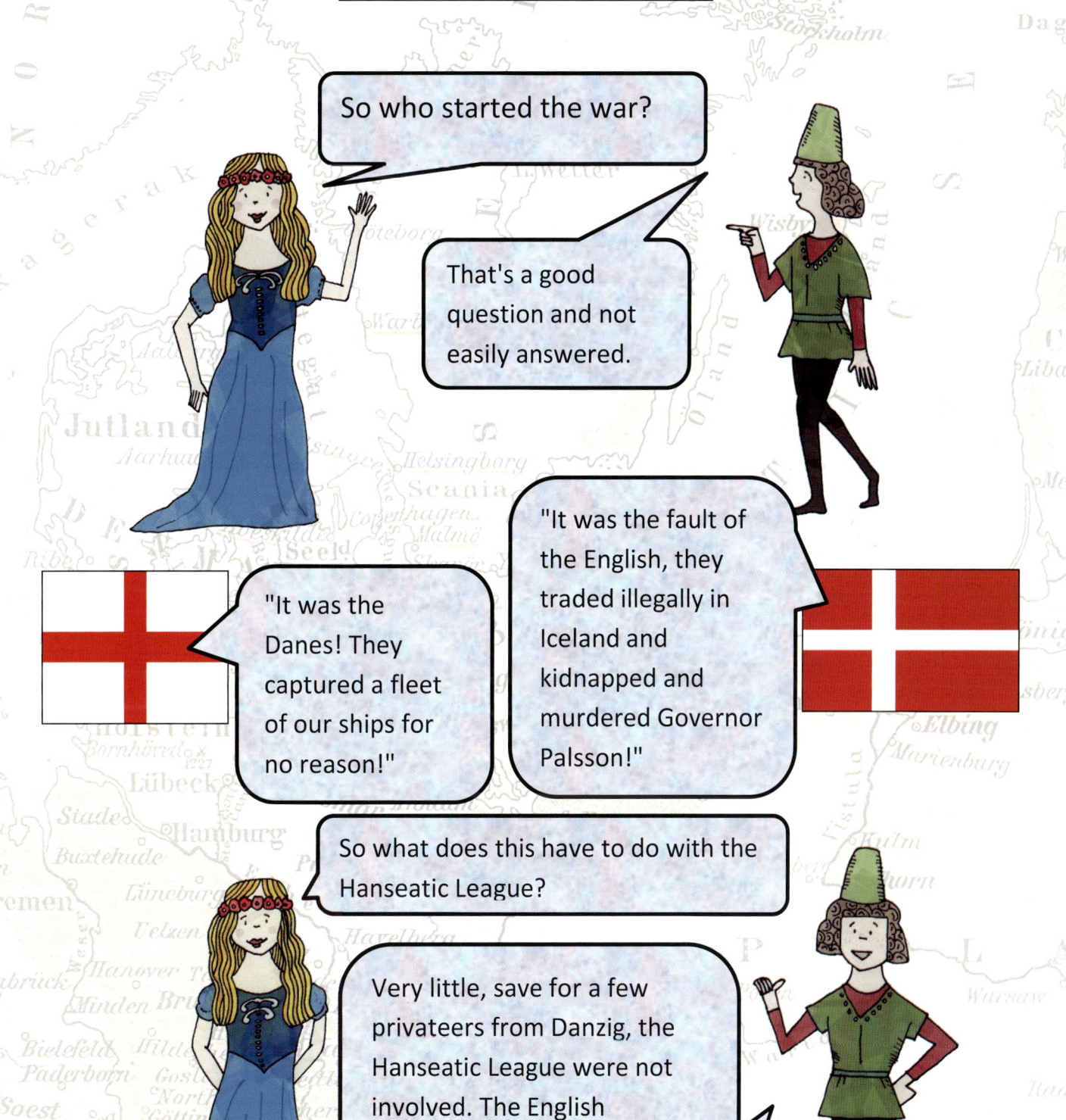

So who started the war?

That's a good question and not easily answered.

"It was the Danes! They captured a fleet of our ships for no reason!"

"It was the fault of the English, they traded illegally in Iceland and kidnapped and murdered Governor Palsson!"

So what does this have to do with the Hanseatic League?

Very little, save for a few privateers from Danzig, the Hanseatic League were not involved. The English government took advantage of the situation and blamed them for the act of piracy.

Did You Know? The result of this was that trade between the English east coast ports and Lübeck, Hamburg, Bremen, Stralsund, Rostock and Danzig was suspended.

They took great offence and in 1468 the Hanse town of Hamburg commissioned privateers Dodrik Pining and Hans Pothorst to attack English merchant ships found in the North Sea.

With little hope for conciliation the naval conflict began in earnest, with merchant vessels being converted into battleships scouring the waves looking for enemy craft. Bruges' Kontor was one of the first to take the initiative and paid for two Danzig vessels to be converted to attack English ships in January 1470.

Although many of the Hanseatic towns endeavoured to remain neutral, as war was already cutting into their profits (Cologne was ejected from the Hanseatic League for refusing to participate). Hamburg, Bremen, Danzig and Lübeck were the most enthusiastic providers of privateers whose owners and crews were naturally hoping to profit from plundering enemy ships.

Image from Forces of the Hanseatic League by David Nicolle © Osprey Publishing Ltd.

Costs of the war

* Losses at sea for the English in the summer 1470 and 1471

* English took four Lübeck privateers in July 1472

* Damage to the economy as unable to trade

* Impact on resources for the English war with France

Did You Know? Given the expense, neither Germans nor English commissioned more than twenty privateers each to fight the enemy.

The Treaty of Utrecht (1474)

One positive thing to come out of the Anglo-Hanseatic Sea War was a strengthening of English ties with Holland. During these war years more fish than usual was imported into Lynn and Boston by the Hollanders and Zeelanders who took corn from the Wash ports. This made the Netherlands an ideal location for the peace talks. They began at Utrecht, roughly 31 miles from the Dutch capital Amsterdam, in July 1473. The English delegation was led by Edward IV's secretary, William Hatclyff, and the head of the German delegation was Heinrich Castorp, the mayor of Lübeck. As mentioned earlier Hamburg and Danzig had pursued the war against England with greater enthusiasm than Lübeck because both cities had lost more in the English confiscation of Hanseatic property in 1468.

The Treaty of Utrecht
February 1474

- Restoration of trade

- German trading privileges restored as per the Treaty of London (1437)

- Reopening of the London Steelyard and reopening of the Boston Kontor and a new Kontor for the Germans in Lynn

- £10,000 compensation (Customs lost during war, exception for staple goods) paid by the English

- All Hanseatic Imports and Exports to be recorded.

It looks like the Germans got the best deal!

So that's how Lynn got a Kontor?

Yes but we know it as The Hanse House!

Did You Know? The Hanse House is the sole surviving Medieval Kontor of the Hanseatic League in England. The two warehouses running down from the street to the river Ouse were developed by the Germans (specifically Danzig, Hamburg and Bremen) after the property came into their possession in 1475.

Hans Holbein the Younger
The Merchant Georg Gisze, 1532, on display at the Germäldergalerie der Staatlichen Museen zu Berlin.

(Not actually Lutkyn as there are no pictures of him)

Meet Lutkyn Smith

Who was he? A German merchant

Where was he from? Hamburg

How long had he been connected to Lynn? 30 years

What was his title? Governor of the Lynn Kontor

Who appointed him? The London Steelyard

When? Before 1500

How many merchants would have been there? In 1500 - 41 merchants based here.

What was Lutkyn importing? Iron, wood and pitch.

51

Hanseatic traders occupied the Lynn Kontor until the 1560's when it was let to Lynn merchants. It had warehouses, wharfs, shops, cellars, yards and gardens. Much like today.

FUN FACT! The Hanse House was sold by the Hanseatic League in 1751 for £800 to Edward Everard. That's about a quarter of a million pounds in today's money!

The Hanse House Today

Chapter Five:
Lynn and the Hanse Today
What is the New Hanseatic League?

> The New Hanseatic League was founded in Zwolle in the Netherlands in 1980 with the intention to reconnect towns across North Europe which had historical ties through the Hanseatic League.

Countries of The New Hanseatic League

Belarus	Latvia
Belgium	Lithuania
England	Netherlands
Estonia	Norway
Finland	Poland
France	Russia
Germany	Scotland
Iceland	Sweden

Did You Know? Today there are 185 member cities with a population of 27 million in 16 countries with German and English as the two official languages.

The Rise of the New Hanseatic League

The rapid growth of the New Hanseatic League was in part a consequence of the fall of the **Iron Curtain** in the 1990's. Town's once in the Hanseatic League in the past could now join the modern urban alliance.

Glossary
Iron Curtain- A political and physical boundary dividing Europe into two separate halves from the end of World War II (1945) until the end of the Cold War (1991).

"So how did Lynn become a member of the New Hanseatic League?"

"In July 2005 the King's Lynn and West Norfolk Borough Council successfully applied for membership of the New Hanseatic League at the annual conference of the member cities in Estonia."

Did You Know? Our representative, Councillor Nick Daubney, travelled to Germany for his first Hanseatic meeting during one of the worst snow storms ever seen in the country but made it there safely. Cementing a union which has lasted over a decade.

"At least he didn't get lice, like poor Margery Kempe!"

The youthHansa

What's the youthHansa?

The youthHansa is the youth organization of the New Hanseatic League. Every year Hanseatic cities send young delegates ranging from 16 to 25 years of age to take part in the delegation meetings of the youthHansa and the Hanseatic Days.

Did You Know? The concept of the youthHansa was introduced for the first time in 1998 when the Hanseatic city of Visby in Sweden invited 16-25 year olds to a youth forum. Everyone had such a good time that the New Hanseatic League decided to invite the young people on a regular basis and this resulted in the founding of the youthHansa.

What does the youthHansa do?

- Promote the exchange of views and experiences concerning youth issues.
- Develop specific youth projects between the Hanseatic cities.
- Promote school partnerships and youth exchanges.
- Improve the mutual understanding between young people from the Hanseatic cities.
- Bring non-organized young people and youth groups together in order to strengthen the sense of community between the Hanseatic cities and their young inhabitants.

The Hanse Festival

The concept of the Hanse Festival in Lynn began in the summer of 1998 as a civic driven event which raised awareness of its Hanseatic heritage through exhibitions, concerts, guides tours and a Symposium or history conference.

Ten years after joining the New Hanseatic League in 2015 the town celebrated this international alliance with a series of events including a fireworks display, a colourful medieval market and bands playing jazz, folk and classical music. A History and Archaeology Symposium, a Community Breakfast and the arrival of a Kogge from the Netherlands were also highlights.

It looks really fun!

Hanse Festival

Business Hanse

The Business Hanse

The new Business Hanse was founded in June 2013 in Herford, Germany with more than 220 participants from 12 countries. The new Business Hanse represent traditional values in modern business life. Its members regard themselves as "respectable merchants" of modern times. In 2014 King's Lynn held its first Hanse Business Convention and followed it with an even larger one in 2015 to celebrate the confirmation of The Borough Council of King's Lynn and West Norfolk becoming the English Office for the Business Hanse, effectively Lynn became a Kontor again.

Activities

King's Lynn and The Hanseatic League Word Search

```
T V C C O A K C P P R D X R V W I P M R
V H O K F B O B Z B K S A E K B O I B U
L G C D F S N F X C M S K J A M W U M N
K Y Q E F I T S Y E Y E P R Y W U L E O
G N N M R V O U G N O I R A J O S Q D T
K W I N U T R V M O R X H C C O D M I S
W S Q G Y R U N I A R G Y E H L I G E O
D O M H H G X C T H X D N B L A H L V B
B F S B I T C E I V I G J P D F N L A K
P I H Z D V E K K F L T U K L S A T L P
F J N H U L L T X A I G X Z M X B R S I
P A F N Y R R Q N L X V N V U R E E V F
D F D G G N F D G O P E E G K U D Q S R
L P J E A S T E R L I N G S J P A S T G
B E W Q Y S D Q Y V N M L I N E R G K D
Y P T G K B Z Z D J Z P Z C A A T W Z P
Y N A M R E G G K E A C O V X F H F Y O
O L W F P N I A A F P J N G A S W E O J
G H X Q U X P L Y K A M P E N M V D Q L
D X N J V R V G E W U U K T P A U O K G
```

Boston	Kampen
Cog	Knight
Danzig	Kontor
Easterlings	Lynn
England	Medieval
Fish	Merchants
Germany	Pirate
Grain	Trade
Hanse	Utrecht

Solution on page 65.

King's Lynn and the Hanseatic League Town Trail

1. King's Lynn Minster
2. Hampton Court
3. Hanse House
4. Marriott's Warehouse
5. The Purfleet
6. King's Lynn Arts Centre
7. St Nicholas' Chapel.

1). Start in Lynn Minster (Saturday Market Place).

Can you find the Hanseatic chest? This would have been used as storage for goods during a sea voyage and then re-used by Lynn merchants to store clothes or items of value.

Go to the memorial brasses in the south-east corner of the church.

Can you find the early example of a post windmill on Adam de Walsoken's and his wife Margaret's brass?

Now have a look at the brass of Robert Braunche and his wives, Letitia and Margaret.

Can you find the lady serving a peacock in the feast scene (this might be easier to see on the rubbing of the brass)? Peacock was a luxury food item and it is probably being served to King Edward III, who visited Lynn in 1348.

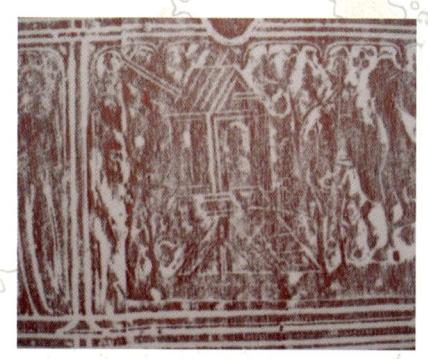

2). Leave the Minster and walk to Nelson Street. Go into the courtyard of Hampton Court (the bright orange building!).

Please remember to be quiet – these are people's homes!

The section of the building you have just walked through and the warehouse range facing you were built in the 15th century – while the Hanseatic merchants were in Lynn. The building on the left is even older, dating to the 14th century, while the building on the right was built later in the 17th century.

The orange colour of the front of the building recreates what it would have looked like in the medieval period.

As you leave – look at the wooden carvings around the door – can you find the merchant mark of the Ampfles family who once lived here. It is a greyhound with an 'A' on its back, which helped people who could not read find the right place.

3). Now walk down St. Margaret's Lane towards the South Quay.
The brick and timber framed building on your right is a warehouse belonging to the Hanse House. It was built by the Hanseatic merchants after the site was given to them by Edward IV following the Treaty of Utrecht in 1474.
It was in these buildings that the merchants would have stored and sold their goods, and also where they would have had their offices, eaten and slept.

4). Walk along the South Quay towards Marriott's Warehouse.

Have a look at the sculpture outside which shows stockfish being dried in the wind in Norway before being sent by Hanseatic merchants to Lynn.

Can you find some of the more unusual fish, like the stingray?

If you go up to the 1st floor of Marriott's Warehouse you can see models of some of Lynn's historic buildings.

Which buildings do you recognise and can you find some of them on the town model?

5). Now leave Marriott's Warehouse and walk along the South Quay to the Custom House. As you walk past the River Great Ouse can you imagine what it would have been like in the medieval period? It was said the river was once so full of ships that you could walk across their decks from one side of the river to the other.

When you reach the Purfleet you have found the main source of drinking water for the medieval population of Lynn. It was also their main method of sewage disposal.

Can you imagine what life would have been like for children living in medieval Lynn?

Can you imagine what it would have smelt like?

6). Cross the Purfleet and walk down King Street (once Stockfish Row) towards the Tuesday Market Place. As you go past St. George's Guildhall (the Arts Centre) have a look at the largest surviving guildhall in England. Today it is used as a theatre, but it has also been used as a stage scenery workshop and a Civil War weapon store.

7). Cross the Tuesday Market Place and walk to St. Nicholas Chapel, the last building on this trail.

This is the largest Chapel-of-Ease in the country and it was built because the medieval population of Lynn was too large for St. Margaret's (now the Minster) to accomodate alone. St. Nicholas is the patron saint of sailors, which made him very popular in this port town.

The Chapel and its spire would have dominated the skyline of medieval Lynn and it was used by returning sailors as a seamark (a visual aid to navigation).

When you go inside make sure you look at the 15th century carved angels in the roof. Can you find the one holding a recorder? This is the earliest known portrayal of the instrument in church carving.

Which of your Lynn ships will reach Lübeck safely?

Congratulations! You have reached Lübeck.

Bad luck! Your ship was sunk in a storm.

Bad luck! Your ship was attacked by pirates.

Hanseaten Biscuits Recipe

Ingredients
300g plain flour
200g cold butter
100g caster sugar
splash of vanilla extract
1 egg
2 tsps strawberry jam
200g icing sugar
red food colouring

Method
1. Mix the flour, butter, sugar, vanilla and egg into a dough.
2. Put the mixture into the fridge for one hour then roll out flat.
3. Cut the circular biscuit shapes and lay on a greased baking tray.
4. Bake for 15 minutes in a preheated oven 200 degrees or Gas mark 6.
5. Remove biscuits from the oven when they are a golden colour and place them on a rack to cool.
6. When the biscuits have cooled warm the jam in a saucepan and apply it to half the biscuits.
7. Put the remaining biscuits on top of the jam covered ones.
8. Make the icing by mixing the icing sugar with cold water (not too much water or the icing will be too runny!).
9. Split the icing into two bowls and add the red colouring to one bowl.
10. Decorate the biscuits with the icing half red, half white – like the picture above.

Instead of decorating your biscuits with red and white icing – try the colours of King's Lynn and use blue and yellow colouring!

Did you Know? Hanseaten are jam filled German biscuits which are often eaten at Christmas.

Word Search Solution

```
T V C C O A K C P P R D X R V W I P M R
V H O K F B O B Z B K S A E K B O I B U
L G C D F S N F X C M S K J A M W U M N
K Y Q E F I T S Y E Y E P R Y W U L E O
G N N M R V O U G N O I R A J O S Q D T
K W I N U T R V M O R X H C C O D M I S
W S Q G Y R U N I A R G Y E H L I G E O
D O M H H G X C T H X D N B L A H L V B
B F S B I T C E I V I G J P D F N L A K
P I H Z D V E K K F L T U K L S A T L P
F J N H U L L T X A I G X Z M X B R S I
P A F N Y R R Q N L X V N V U R E E V F
D F D G G N F D G O P E E G K U D Q S R
L P J E A S T E R L I N G S J P A S T G
B E W Q Y S D Q Y V N M L I N E R G K D
Y P T G K B Z Z D J Z P Z C A A T W Z P
Y N A M R E G G K E A C O V X F H F Y O
O L W F P N I A A F P J N G A S W E O J
G H X Q U X P L Y K A M P E N M V D Q L
D X N J V R V G E W U U K T P A U O K G
```

German Vocabulary

German Word	How to say it	Meaning
Auf Wiedersehen	Ow-f Vee-der-zain	Goodbye
Bin	Bin	Am
Danke	Dan-ka	Thanks
Deutsch	Doyt-ch	German
Dich	Di-sh	You
Ein Fisch	Eye-n Fi-sh	A Fish
Das Getreide	Da-ss Ger-try-der	The Grain
Guten Tag	Goo-ten Tahk	Good day
Habe	Har-ber	Have
Die Hanse	Dee Han-zer	The Hanse
Ein Haus	Eye-n H-ow-s	A House
Ich	ick	I
Ja	Yar	Yes
Ein Junge	Eye-n Yoon-geh	A Boy
Der Kaufmann	D-air Kow-f-man	Merchant
Die Kogge	Dee Cog-er	The Cog
Liebe	Lee-ber	Love
Ein Mädchen	Eye-n M-air-d-ken	A Girl
Nein	Nine	No
Die Stadt	Dee Sht-dat	The Town
Wohne	Voh-ner	Live

Guten tag. Ich bin Nicholas!

Ich wohne in King's Lynn. Ich habe ein Haus in die Stadt.

Did You Know? In German there are 3 words for 'the' (der, die and das) and 2 for 'a' or 'an' (ein and eine). It depends if a word is male, female or neuter. This is called the word's gender. Confusingly 'girl' in German is neuter!

Glossary

Word	Meaning
Absence	To be gone.
Apprentices	Young people learning a particular craft.
Archive	A collection of historic documents.
Bailiff	An officer who collects money owed.
Beheaded/Decapitating	Removal of a head.
Buboes	Inflammation of the lymph nodes in the armpit and groin.
Burgess	Someone in a town or borough with full rights of citizenship.
Carrier	A person who has a disease but suffers no symptoms.
Catalysed	To start or trigger an event.
Cog	Ships with a single mast and a square sail [German – Kogge]
Commercial	A business which makes money.
Commercial Privileges	Special benefits like paying less tax.
Compensation	Money given as a formal apology.
Constitution	A set of rules which organise how a state or group is governed.
Crusader	A Christian knight who fought in the Crusades to claim Jerusalem.
Dunnage	Waste material used to secure cargo on a journey.
Executioner	Person paid to legally kill people.
Export	Sending goods to another country to sell.
Flemings	From Northern Belgium.
Friars	Members of Christian religious orders. Unlike monks they went into the community to preach.
Gotland	Sweden's largest island.
Hanse	A group of people who travel together for safety. Also a common name for the Hanseatic League.

Hinterland	Areas beyond a coastal district or river banks.
Import	Binging goods in from abroad to sell.
Iron Curtain	A political and physical boundary dividing Europe into two separate halves from the end of World War II (1945) until the end of the Cold War (1991).
Kontor	A foreign trading post of the Haseatic League, which contained offices, storage and living space.
Medieval	Also known as the Middle Ages this commonly refers to the period in European history between AD 600 and AD 1500.
Mercenaries	Soldiers for hire.
Merchants	People who buy and sell things made by others for a profit.
Pilgrimage	A journey to visit a religious site or object.
Pitch	A substance used to waterproof wooden ships
Privateers	Legal pirates.
Prussia	An area of Northern Europe now part of Germany and Poland.
Relics	Objects connected to religious figures; such as bones, blood or wood (from Jesus' cross).
Sacked	To attack a city.
Scourge	A menace.
Senate	A political governing body.
Shrines	Holy places dedicated to someone (usually religious).
Steelyard	The name for the main trading post of the Hanseatic League in London.
Tax	An added cost to goods which has to be paid to the government.
Teutonic	German people or things.
Trading Privileges	Better treatment and deals.
Tributaries	Small rivers which flow into larger rivers.
Vittles	Food and other supplies.

Selected Bibliography

Campbell, L. et al. (2006) *King's Lynn The First Thousand Years: A short history by the King's Lynn Blue Badge Guides*, 3rd Ed. King's Lynn Town Guides

Champion, M. (2015) *Medieval Graffiti: The Lost Voices of England's Churches*, London: Ebury Press

Friedland, K. and Richards, P. (ed.) (2005) *Essays in Hanseatic History: The King's Lynn Symposium 1998*, Larks Press

Grant, S. (1995) *Margery Kempe Mystic of Lynn*, Larks Press

Kempe, M. (2004) *The Book of Margery Kempe* [eBook version], translated by B. A. Windeatt, Penguin Books Ltd, available at http://www.amazon.co.uk/gp/product/B002RI97XO?psc=1&redirect=true&ref_=oh_aui_search_detailpage [Accessed 22nd April 2012]

Nicolle, D. (2014) *Forces of the Hanseatic League*, Osprey Publishing Ltd

Nicolle, D. (2007) *Teutonic Knight*, Osprey Publishing Ltd

Richards, P. (2006) *King's Lynn,* Phillimore & Co Ltd

For more information about the New Hanseatic League visit www.hanse.org/en/

Special mention

Dr Paul Richards has kindly allowed us to use information from his forthcoming book *King's Lynn and The Hanseatic League* to be published in 2016.

Acknowledgements

The authors would like to extend their thanks to the following people for their help and support during this project.

The staff and pupils of Eastgate Academy, Reffley Community School and Whitefriars Church of England Primary Academy, for their assistance, enthusiasm and ideas.

The Mayors of Boston, Hamburg, Kampen, King's Lynn and Lübeck for their letters to the children of King's Lynn.

The Borough Council of King's Lynn and West Norfolk, in particular Councillor Nick Daubney, for their interest and support.

All those who generously provided images for this book.

Dr Paul Richards, without whom this book may never have been written.

Thank you to all our sponsors and they are-

King's Lynn Hanseatic Club

King's Lynn Town Guides

Marriott's Warehouse Trust

Sir Jeremy Bagge

The Audrey Stratford Charitable Trust

The Charity of William Cleave

West Norfolk Partnership

List of Illustrations

Page 1: Image of the King's Lynn Coat of Arms used with kind permission of The Borough Council of King's Lynn & West Norfolk Tourism Section.

Page 4. Hanse Festival Fireworks and Kamper Kogge. Images courtesy of The King's Lynn and West Norfolk Borough Council.

Pages 13, 18 & 19: Hansa Map - Plate 28 of Professor G. Droysens Allgemeiner Historische Handatlas, published by R. Andrée, 1886. Also used as watermark throughout.

Pages 15 & 20: Shepherd, William R. *Historical Atlas*, (New York: Barnes and Noble, 1929).

Pages 22 & 23: Trading Goods images by Isobel Rees and Timothy Rees.

Page 23: Image of Jetton used with kind permission of West Norfolk and King's Lynn Archaeological Society © 2013.

Page 25: Robert Braunch memorial brass, Lynn Minster, by Rebecca Rees.

Page 28: Image of Pilgrim Badges used with kind permission of Lynn Museum, Norfolk Museums Service.

Page 30: The Lenn Ship: King's Lynn Borough Archives: KL/C 2/35, image courtesy of the Norfolk Record Office.

Page 31: Image of Ship Graffiti from St. Margaret's Church, Cley next the Sea, Norfolk, courtesy Norfolk Medieval Graffiti Survey.

Page 34: Image of Map from Wikipedia. Image in the public domain.

Page 46 Image of the Execution of Klaus Störtebeker from http://www.cindyvallar.com/death.html

Page 49: Image from *Forces of the Hanseatic League* by David Nicolle © Osprey Publishing Ltd. Illustrator: Gerry Embleton

Page 51: *The Merchant Georg Gisze,* by Hans Holbein the Younger (1532), on display at the Gemäldegalerie der Staatlichen Museen zu Berlin.

Page 52: Images of The Hanse House courtesy of True's Yard Fisherfolk Museum.

Page 56: Festival Images courtesy of The Borough Council of King's Lynn & West Norfolk.

Page 58: Map of the Town Centre used with kind permission of The Borough Council of King's Lynn & West Norfolk Tourism Section.

Pages 59-62: Children's Trail Images by Rebecca Rees.

Page 60: Image of the Hanse House used with kind permission of Kirsty Gauntley, The Hanse House.

Illustrations by Julian Mosedale.

About the Authors

Lindsey Bavin:

Born in Lynn, Lindsey went to school at King Edward VII. She moved away in 2004 to study for her BA Hons in Ancient History and Archaeology and MA in Myth and Ancient Society. In 2012 she became involved with True's Yard Fisherfolk Museum through volunteering and worked her way up to becoming the manager of the Museum. Lindsey is also a trustee of The Marriott's Warehouse Trust.

Rebecca Rees:

Rebecca was born in King's Lynn and went to school in the town. She studied at Newcastle University for a BA Hons. in Classical Studies and an MA in Heritage Education and Interpretation. She is Project Manager for The Marriott's Warehouse Trust and a member of the King's Lynn Town Guides.